HAL•LEONARD
INSTRUMENTAL
PLAY-ALONG

AUDIO
ACCESS
INCLUDED

**PLAYBACK+**
Speed • Pitch • Balance • Loop

# CLARINET

# Jazz Classics

Audio arrangements by Peter Deneff

To access audio visit:
**www.halleonard.com/mylibrary**
Enter Code
7171-6186-7570-3624

ISBN 978-1-4950-4748-0

7777 W. BLUEMOUND RD. P.O. BOX 13819 MILWAUKEE, WI 53213

Visit Hal Leonard Online at
**www.halleonard.com**

# DOXY

Clarinet

By SONNY ROLLINS

**Medium Swing**

# IN WALKED BUD

Clarinet

By THELONIOUS MONK

# IN YOUR OWN SWEET WAY

Clarinet

By DAVE BRUBECK

# MERCY, MERCY, MERCY

CLARINET

Composed by JOSEF ZAWINUL

# NARDIS

CLARINET

By MILES DAVIS

# ON GREEN DOLPHIN STREET

**Clarinet**

Lyrics by NED WASHINGTON
Music by BRONISLAU KAPER

**D.S. al Coda**

# REUNION BLUES

CLARINET

By MILT JACKSON

# STOLEN MOMENTS

Clarinet

Words and Music by
OLIVER NELSON

# ST. THOMAS

Clarinet

By SONNY ROLLINS

# SCRAPPLE FROM THE APPLE

CLARINET

By CHARLIE PARKER

D.S. al Fine

# SIDEWINDER

Clarinet

By LEE MORGAN

# TAKE FIVE

Clarinet

By PAUL DESMOND

D.S. al Coda

# HAL•LEONARD INSTRUMENTAL PLAY-ALONG

Your favorite songs are arranged just for solo instrumentalists with this outstanding series. Each book includes a great full-accompaniment play-along audio so you can sound just like a pro! Check out **www.halleonard.com** to see all the titles available.

## The Beatles

All You Need Is Love • Blackbird • Day Tripper • Eleanor Rigby • Get Back • Here, There and Everywhere • Hey Jude • I Will • Let It Be • Lucy in the Sky with Diamonds • Ob-La-Di, Ob-La-Da • Penny Lane • Something • Ticket to Ride • Yesterday.

| | | | |
|---|---|---|---|
| _____ | 00225330 | Flute | $14.99 |
| _____ | 00225331 | Clarinet | $14.99 |
| _____ | 00225332 | Alto Sax | $14.99 |
| _____ | 00225333 | Tenor Sax | $14.99 |
| _____ | 00225334 | Trumpet | $14.99 |
| _____ | 00225335 | Horn | $14.99 |
| _____ | 00225336 | Trombone | $14.99 |
| _____ | 00225337 | Violin | $14.99 |
| _____ | 00225338 | Viola | $14.99 |
| _____ | 00225339 | Cello | $14.99 |

## Chart Hits

All About That Bass • All of Me • Happy • Radioactive • Roar • Say Something • Shake It Off • A Sky Full of Stars • Someone like You • Stay with Me • Thinking Out Loud • Uptown Funk.

| | | | |
|---|---|---|---|
| _____ | 00146207 | Flute | $12.99 |
| _____ | 00146208 | Clarinet | $12.99 |
| _____ | 00146209 | Alto Sax | $12.99 |
| _____ | 00146210 | Tenor Sax | $12.99 |
| _____ | 00146211 | Trumpet | $12.99 |
| _____ | 00146212 | Horn | $12.99 |
| _____ | 00146213 | Trombone | $12.99 |
| _____ | 00146214 | Violin | $12.99 |
| _____ | 00146215 | Viola | $12.99 |
| _____ | 00146216 | Cello | $12.99 |

## Coldplay

Clocks • Every Teardrop Is a Waterfall • Fix You • In My Place • Lost! • Paradise • The Scientist • Speed of Sound • Trouble • Violet Hill • Viva La Vida • Yellow.

| | | | |
|---|---|---|---|
| _____ | 00103337 | Flute | $12.99 |
| _____ | 00103338 | Clarinet | $12.99 |
| _____ | 00103339 | Alto Sax | $12.99 |
| _____ | 00103340 | Tenor Sax | $12.99 |
| _____ | 00103341 | Trumpet | $12.99 |
| _____ | 00103342 | Horn | $12.99 |
| _____ | 00103343 | Trombone | $12.99 |
| _____ | 00103344 | Violin | $12.99 |
| _____ | 00103345 | Viola | $12.99 |
| _____ | 00103346 | Cello | $12.99 |

## Disney Greats

Arabian Nights • Hawaiian Roller Coaster Ride • It's a Small World • Look Through My Eyes • Yo Ho (A Pirate's Life for Me) • and more.

| | | | |
|---|---|---|---|
| _____ | 00841934 | Flute | $12.99 |
| _____ | 00841935 | Clarinet | $12.99 |
| _____ | 00841936 | Alto Sax | $12.99 |
| _____ | 00841937 | Tenor Sax | $12.95 |
| _____ | 00841938 | Trumpet | $12.99 |
| _____ | 00841939 | Horn | $12.99 |
| _____ | 00841940 | Trombone | $12.95 |
| _____ | 00841941 | Violin | $12.99 |
| _____ | 00841942 | Viola | $12.99 |
| _____ | 00841943 | Cello | $12.99 |
| _____ | 00842078 | Oboe | $12.99 |

## Great Themes

Bella's Lullaby • Chariots of Fire • Get Smart • Hawaii Five-O Theme • I Love Lucy • The Odd Couple • Spanish Flea • and more.

| | | | |
|---|---|---|---|
| _____ | 00842468 | Flute | $12.99 |
| _____ | 00842469 | Clarinet | $12.99 |
| _____ | 00842470 | Alto Sax | $12.99 |
| _____ | 00842471 | Tenor Sax | $12.99 |
| _____ | 00842472 | Trumpet | $12.99 |
| _____ | 00842473 | Horn | $12.99 |
| _____ | 00842474 | Trombone | $12.99 |
| _____ | 00842475 | Violin | $12.99 |
| _____ | 00842476 | Viola | $12.99 |
| _____ | 00842477 | Cello | $12.99 |

## Popular Hits

Breakeven • Fireflies • Halo • Hey, Soul Sister • I Gotta Feeling • I'm Yours • Need You Now • Poker Face • Viva La Vida • You Belong with Me • and more.

| | | | |
|---|---|---|---|
| _____ | 00842511 | Flute | $12.99 |
| _____ | 00842512 | Clarinet | $12.99 |
| _____ | 00842513 | Alto Sax | $12.99 |
| _____ | 00842514 | Tenor Sax | $12.99 |
| _____ | 00842515 | Trumpet | $12.99 |
| _____ | 00842516 | Horn | $12.99 |
| _____ | 00842517 | Trombone | $12.99 |
| _____ | 00842518 | Violin | $12.99 |
| _____ | 00842519 | Viola | $12.99 |
| _____ | 00842520 | Cello | $12.99 |

## Songs from Frozen, Tangled and Enchanted

Do You Want to Build a Snowman? • For the First Time in Forever • Happy Working Song • I See the Light • In Summer • Let It Go • Mother Knows Best • That's How You Know • True Love's First Kiss • When Will My Life Begin • and more.

| | | | |
|---|---|---|---|
| _____ | 00126921 | Flute | $14.99 |
| _____ | 00126922 | Clarinet | $14.99 |
| _____ | 00126923 | Alto Sax | $14.99 |
| _____ | 00126924 | Tenor Sax | $14.99 |
| _____ | 00126925 | Trumpet | $14.99 |
| _____ | 00126926 | Horn | $14.99 |
| _____ | 00126927 | Trombone | $14.99 |
| _____ | 00126928 | Violin | $14.99 |
| _____ | 00126929 | Viola | $14.99 |
| _____ | 00126930 | Cello | $14.99 |

## Top Hits

Adventure of a Lifetime • Budapest • Die a Happy Man • Ex's & Oh's • Fight Song • Hello • Let It Go • Love Yourself • One Call Away • Pillowtalk • Stitches • Writing's on the Wall.

| | | | |
|---|---|---|---|
| _____ | 00171073 | Flute | $12.99 |
| _____ | 00171074 | Clarinet | $12.99 |
| _____ | 00171075 | Alto Sax | $12.99 |
| _____ | 00171106 | Tenor Sax | $12.99 |
| _____ | 00171107 | Trumpet | $12.99 |
| _____ | 00171108 | Horn | $12.99 |
| _____ | 00171109 | Trombone | $12.99 |
| _____ | 00171110 | Violin | $12.99 |
| _____ | 00171111 | Viola | $12.99 |
| _____ | 00171112 | Cello | $12.99 |

## Wicked

As Long As You're Mine • Dancing Through Life • Defying Gravity • For Good • I'm Not That Girl • Popular • The Wizard and I • and more.

| | | | |
|---|---|---|---|
| _____ | 00842236 | Flute | $12.99 |
| _____ | 00842237 | Clarinet | $12.99 |
| _____ | 00842238 | Alto Saxophone | $11.95 |
| _____ | 00842239 | Tenor Saxophone | $11.95 |
| _____ | 00842240 | Trumpet | $11.99 |
| _____ | 00842241 | Horn | $11.95 |
| _____ | 00842242 | Trombone | $12.99 |
| _____ | 00842243 | Violin | $11.99 |
| _____ | 00842244 | Viola | $12.99 |
| _____ | 00842245 | Cello | $12.99 |

HAL•LEONARD®

0617